4 SIMPLE HIDDEN WAYS TO MAKE MONEY ONLINE THROUGH AMAZON

Julius Adeolotu

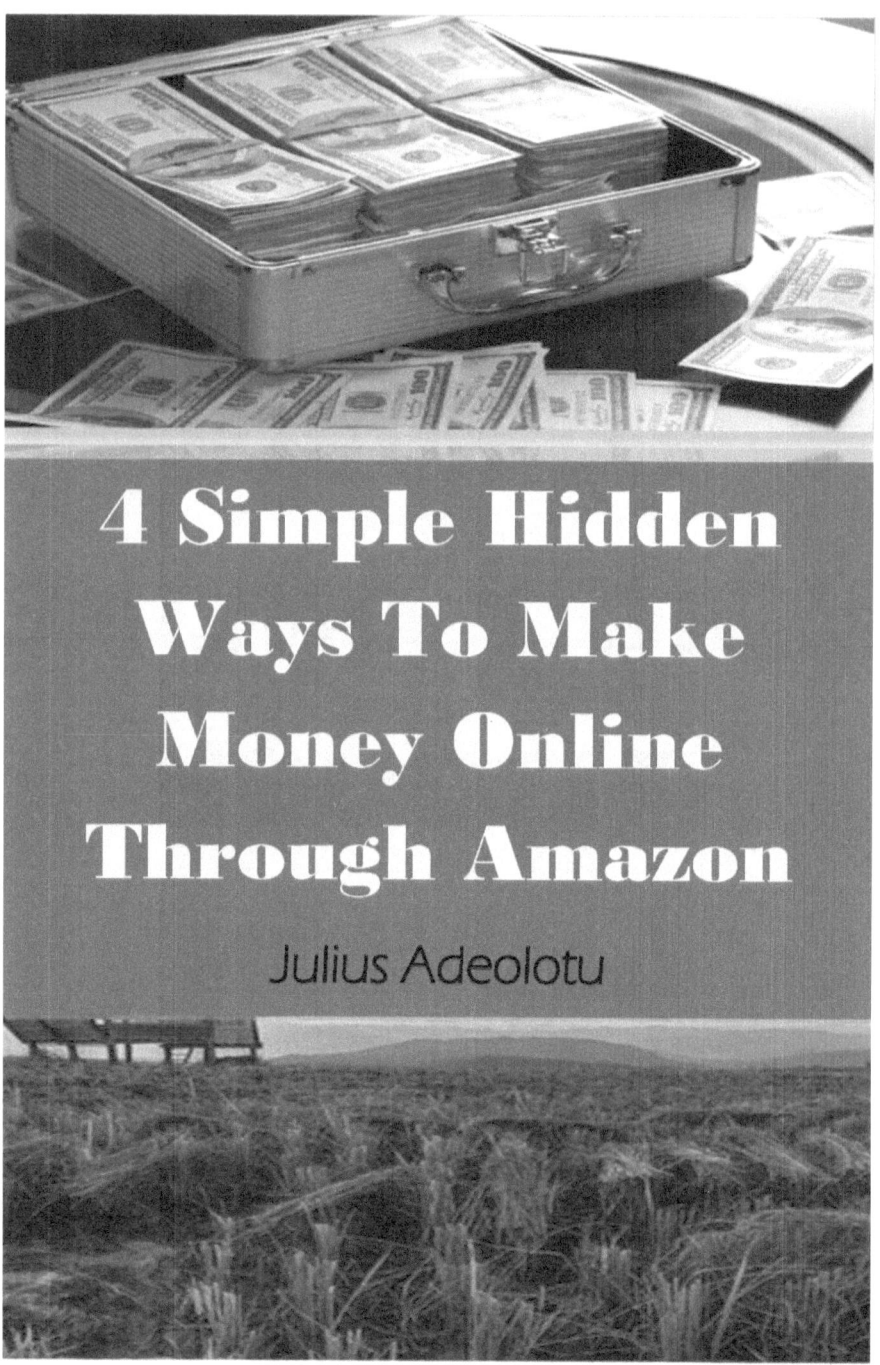

4 Simple Hidden Ways To Make Money Online Through Amazon

Julius Adeolotu

COPYRIGHT

No part of this book should be used in any form without an express written permission from the author.

In case of any reference to any content in this book, adequate reference must be made.

TABLE OF CONTENTS

Title page	1 - 2
Copyright	3
Dedication	5
Introduction	6 - 8
Chapter one: Overview Of the 4 Methods	9 - 11
Chapter Two: All You Need To Have To Make Money Online	12-14
Chapter Three: Method 1	15 - 21
Chapter Four: Method Two	22 - 24
Chapter Five: Method Three	25 - 29
Chapter Six: Method Four	30 - 33
Chapter Seven: A special Bonus Chapter	34 - 35
Conclusion	36
Other Books by the Author.	

DEDICATION

This book is dedicated to you. Yes, you for taking out time and the desire to change your financial situations.

INTRODUCTION

4 Simple Hidden Ways to make money online through Amazon Shows You the Exact Time tested and trusted way of making money online from hoe without any stress. It is a completely beginners and Newbie Friendly guide. It showcases the exact Blue Print I and other top Internet Marketers daily Use to make a Killing making endless money online. It is a simplified step by step guide of making money online through Amazon. It is a simple yet hidden system of how to make money Online. This book is guaranteed to make you have your Own Home-Based Business!

(Take Note Please: You can start **making money online immediately** after reading this guide if you decide to. I'm about to show you how.)

4 Simple Hidden ways To Make Money Online Through Amazon is a simple step-by-step guide on how to start making money online immediately with **nothing absolutely** and build for yourself an enviable life transforming online business empire that will freely give you all the freedom you can ever dream of having!

With this book, I have successfully come up with a solid system that is guaranteed never to fail in your bid to making money online from the comfort of your home without pressures or hassles from a boss. You have with you a failure-proof game plan that anyone, irrespective of his age or level of education can use to go from the level of having nothing or beginning with virtually no single dime to making a full time living on the internet through the platform of Amazon. 4 Simple Hidden ways to make money online is the method I have used without any regrets to crave a living for myself online. The teachings in this book have allowed me to joyfully resign from my over-demanding, stressful and boring job. I have been able to concentrate fully on making money online through Amazon and with this; I have achieved the true financial freedom I have always dreamt of having. You too will have all these and much more for yourself as a result of applying the teachings in this online money making book. The beauty of this is that it is fully home based —so you work from the comfort of your home.

This book has in it a great measure of valuable and life transforming knowledge that is dead simple to implement and start seeing immediate results as you will have powerful results from implementing the tips! I have laid bare to you in simple terms all the tips and techniques I and other fellow world acclaimed internet business owners are using on a daily basis to build financial fortune for themselves online.

This book comes with four simple and hidden ways of how to make money online through Amazon. Each method is simple and easy to digest with guarantee of making you instant money online if you take immediate action. You might be broke at the moment but you should never allow yourself to remain broke. This book gives you the tool and knowledge to break free financially. I simply advise to get started with the money making ideas shared in this book and you will see yourself a living testimony of how to make money on the internet through Amazon. All of the topics I cover in this money making book are mind blowing. They include what you never expected.

I have also included an additional special bonus chapter in addition to the four ways of making money online via Amazon.

It doesn't count if you're a newbie in the Internet world or have struggled fruitlessly all in a bid to make money online. All you need is the right attitude! With your desire to make money online, you are assured of having a living online if only you follow my blue prints in this book

The Internet is filled with numerous opportunities of making money online! People make a living online and get richer everyday working online from the comfort of their homes! The main difference between you and them is you haven't discovered a way to make money online for yourself. All that is coming to an end today. With this book, you now have an edge and you can make money online for yourself. Get started right way by clicking the "**Buy**" button.

CHAPTER ONE

OVERVIEW OF THE FOUR METHODS OF MAKING MONEY ONLINE

Amazon is one of the most visited websites in the world. As a matter of fact, it is the largest ecommerce site in the world with billions of transactions being carried out on it on daily basis.

Amazon can be regarded as an-everything store. With the large database of different items, there is virtually nothing you are looking for that you will not find on Amazon. Be it books, electronics, technological gadgets, house hold appliances, groceries, clothes, etc, you just name it. You have everything available for sale on Amazon.

Amazon is the number one go to place for all your shopping.

Making Money on Amazon?

Many have wondered how possible it is to make money on Amazon. Little did they know that the answer is not farfetched from them? There are millions of individuals globally who are making endless amount of money in various currencies from Amazon.

Have you ever wondered how to make money online from Amazon?

Are you even interested in having your own share of the billions of dollars being shared on Amazon?

Have you ever searched for Amazon on how to make easily money online?

Have you?

Have you...?

Have you ...?

Whatever might have been your puzzle and questions about making money online, I don't care. I only care about you making real genuine money on the internet via the Amazon platform. I have gotten a piece of good news for you. I want you to sit back and relax as I ride you through the journey of making money online from Amazon.

Here is the general outline of what this make money online guide will show you:

Method 1: Selling of your Products.

Method 2: Creating an Amazon web store

Method 3: Displaying and showcasing Amazon adverts on your online web presence

Method 4: Publishing your books

Bonus Chapter: Becoming an Amazon affiliate

Are you ready to go?
Oh Yes! I can hear you scream.
Let's get started then.

CHAPTER TWO: ALL YOU NEED TO HAVE TO MAKE MONEY ONLINE

You already have what it takes to make money online by the virtue of you buying and reading this book.

The first and most essential ingredient you need in order to make money online is to have the **_DESIRE._**

The beginning of any great and worthwhile achievement in life starts with desire. Desire is the beginning of any true online money making venture. Since you have the desire to make money online via Amazon, I can assure you that you will make money online.

Moreover, here is a list of other things you will need in order to make money online, most importantly on Amazon.

1. Passion
2. Determination
3. Diligence
4. Persistence
5. Dedication
6. Tactics
7. Continuous quest for updated knowledge
8. Tenacity
9. An internet enabled device
10. Good communication skills (written most especially)
11. An eagle eye.
12. Ability to spot ready markets.

CHAPTER THREE: METHOD 1

SELLING YOUR PRODUCTS ON AMAZON

In your bid on how to make money online, the subject of selling can never be downgraded. You can never ignore the skill of selling in order to make money for yourself. As it is in the offline world, so it is on the online market (the World Wide Web).

Selling is an essential skill in making money online. On the subject of making money on Amazon, you can never downplay on the aspect of selling. As a matter of fact, the easiest way to make money via Amazon is to have something to sell.

Selling products online is one of the quickest and easiest ways to make money online.

What can I sell on Amazon?

Having established the fact that selling is one of the simplest ways to make money online, what then can be sold online?

What then can I sell on Amazon in order for me to make money online?

rightly believe that that's the questions of most of you reading this now.

What can I sell on Amazon in order to make money online?

Here in this section, I will be exposing to you what you can sell on Amazon that will pull in huge profits thereby certifying you as someone who makes money online.

Here is a fact: **There is no limit to what you can sell on Amazon in order to make money online.**

Yes, you just read that right.

You mean what?

I repeat: **There is no limit to what you can sell on Amazon in order to make money online.**

There is no limit to what you can sell on Amazon in order to make money online.

There is no limit to what you can sell on Amazon in order to make money online.

There is no limit to what you can sell on Amazon in order to make money online.

You can, as a matter of fact, sell anything sellable on Amazon.

Here is an inexhaustible list of what you can sell on Amazon in order to make money online for yourself:

1. Clothes
2. Shoes
3. Movies, Music and games
4. Electronics
5. Computers
6. Computer accessories
7. Office equipments
8. Groceries
9. Home appliances
10. Pets
11. Garden
12. Tools
13. Beauty products
14. Health products
15. Household items

16. Toys
17. Kids items
18. Baby items
19. Jewelry
20. Handmade items
21. Sports items
22. Outdoor items
23. Automotive
24. Industrial appliances
25. Home services
26. Etc

The list is just endless.

The beauty of selling on Amazon in order to make money online is that you are riding on the legacy built by Amazon. Amazon in over the years has built on its reputation as a global brand. Hence, it has tons of traffic as there are millions of users on its platform worldwide. So, you have ready market for your products irrespective of the item, niches or conditions.

One thing to note is that Amazon charges you $0.99 for every item you sell online on its platform. You can equally sell used or new products.

What to do to get started selling on Amazon

All you need do is to sign up as a seller.

There are two options for you as a seller on Amazon:

1. Individual seller

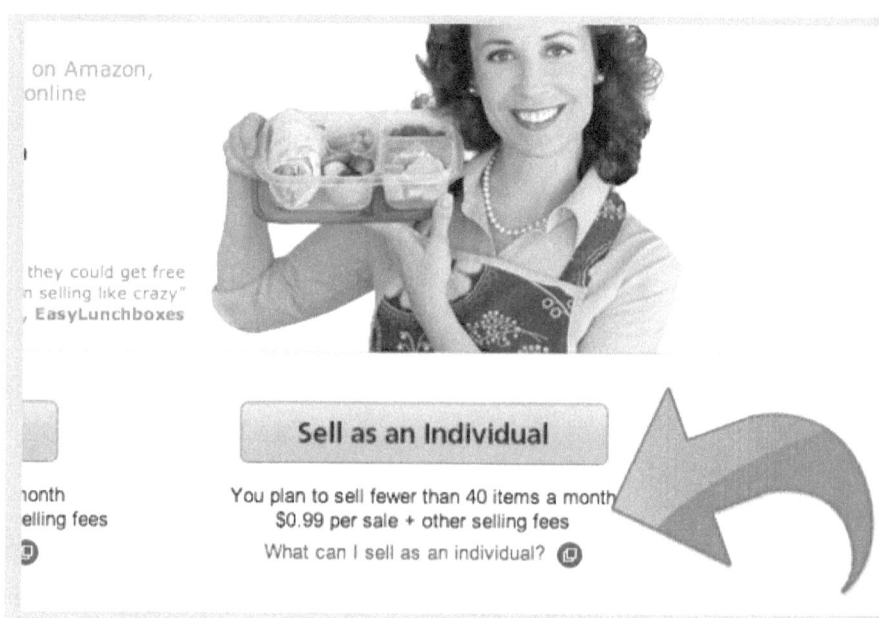

2. Professional seller

It is advisable to register as a professional seller if you intending many and various items.

CHAPTER FOUR: METHOD TWO

BUILD AN AMAZON WEBSTORE ACCOUNT

Another method to make money online is for you to have an e-commerce website or a mini e-commerce store. With an e-commerce store, you have a web presence for your commodities to be viewed and purchased online 24/7 without any limitation.

In this guide on how to make money on Amazon, the second method we are looking at in your bid to make money online is for you to leverage on the reputation and traffic of Amazon as an e-commerce and technology giants to drive massive sales to your goods and commodities.

All that is needed for you is to create a store under the Amazon platform.

How is this done?

With Amazon web store, you don't need to be a tech guru to implement your online store in your bid to make money online. It's as simple as ABC.

With Amazon's robust technology in place, the hard side of listing your store online in order to make money online has been catered for. All you have to do is to have your ecommerce website built and designed with the assistance made available by Amazon.

CHAPTER FIVE: METHOD THREE

ADVERTISE ONLINE

This is another simple way of making money online with Amazon. It has already been established that Amazon, as a tech and ecommerce giant has a lot of traffic to its platforms. It can easily boast of daily billion visits from all across the globe. At such, smart business owners and companies have seen Amazon as a veritable and efficient way to reach to global audience and targets.

How?

It's simply through the way of advertisements. Millions of businesses and companies in the globe pay and beg Amazon to let them advertise their products on its platform so that they can reach out to potential customers and clients. So, Amazon agrees and offers to display their adverts on its websites in view to millions of people across the globe.

But there is a loophole somewhere.

Amazon can never contain all the adverts companies in the world pay them to adverts their goods and services on their platform. So, what do they do?

They can't ignore nor reject the offer of these companies since they pay them massively.

So Amazon thought it wise to partner with individuals like you.

Here is the catch. You simply allow Amazon to display those adverts on your sites of companies that pay them to display on Amazon platform.

Did you get that?

Oh, it's just that simple.

All you ne3ed to do is to craft enticing adverts on your sites and then drive enough traffic to your site in order to increase your earnings. With this, you can make huge amount of money online via your partnership with Amazon.

The more your traffic, the more your revenue.

The huge your traffic, the huge your earnings will be.

The more people you drive to your website, the more money you make online.

The limitless the traffic to your website is, the limitless the money you make will become.

So, my simple advice is to see to it that you drive good enough traffic to your website in order to make more money for yourself online.

Another way to make money online via adverts on Amazon

Another way you can use to make money online by Amazon's advertisements is to select products you desire to advertise on Amazon. I strongly advise that you go with popular and user friendly products that consumers will easily find interesting and attractive. When this is done, you just have to set up a budget for the fee for cost per click (CPC). Then, you sit back and watch how money enters your account.

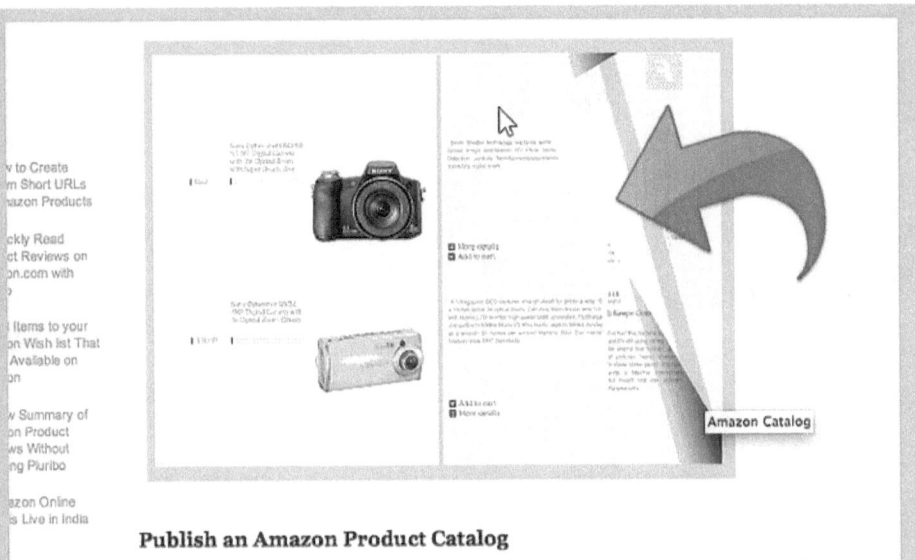

Publish an Amazon Product Catalog

CHAPTER SIX: METHOD FOUR

PUBLISHING BOOKS

Book publishing is one of the times tested and trusted ways of making money on online. When it comes to making money online via the Amazon platform, book publishing is the way to go.

When it comes to making money online via book publishing, then Amazon is the most effective and profitable way to go as it offers the largest record of readership base.

Yes, Amazon is the largest online store for books – both eBooks and paperback books.

Things to note in making money online via Amazon book publishing.

1. In making money online via Amazon publishing, all you need is to be a creative writer and have an unquenchable thirst and passion towards writing.
2. Strive to create values via your published books.
3. Keep writing.
4. Do a thorough market research

5. Go with the niches that sell.

Platforms to use in Amazon publishing

There are two platforms you can use to publish your books on Amazon, both e-books and paperback books. They are:

1. Wwww.kdp.amazon.com
2. www.createspace .com

These two platforms are owned by Amazon and offer the potential of make you huge money online via publishing as they have billions of users on them. The beauty of these platforms is that it is free to sign up and have your books published. Amazon even goes the extra mile to market and distribute your books to readers across the globe. There are countless cases of individuals, including myself, who make money online via Amazon book publishing.

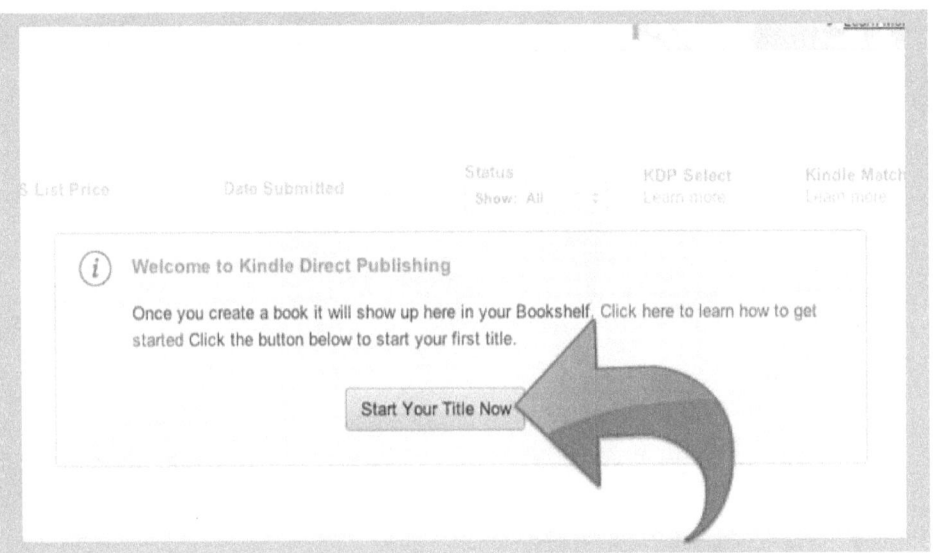

To begin making money via publishing on Amazon, simply go over to the listed Amazon and create space websites above and create an account there.

CHAPTER SEVEN: SPECIAL BONUS CHAPTER

BECOMING AN AMZON AFFILIATE

In becoming an Amazon affiliate, all you are required to do is to partner with Amazon. The way you do this is by signing up and allowing Amazon's advertisement to be displayed on your website. The advertisements of Amazon's products will be displayed on your website.

How do I make money with this?

You can easily make money with this as an Amazon affiliate when customers visit your website and make purchases of Amazon's products through your website. Amazon will always pay you an advertising fee who customers who pay visits to Amazon website through your website.

The only condition that is required of you to earn more money more as an Amazon affiliate is for you to drive massive traffic to your website. When the traffic to Amazon's website from your website is huge, you are guaranteed of a substantial income to yourself. The potentials of making money online as an Amazon affiliate are huge as you can earn as high as 10% of the cost of a single product on Amazon that is made possible through your website or blog. This gets better as there is and indexing of the number of products sold via your website or blog. So the more the quantities of products sold, the more money you make online via Amazon as an Amazon affiliate.

CONCLUSION

So there you have it! Go out right away and start implementing all you have learnt in this guide.

I see your struggles ending soon. I see you living the kind of life you've always dreamt of. You will become the next testimony of making money online from the comfort of your home.

Don't forget to check out my other life transforming books.
You will succeed.
Bye.

www.ingramcontent.com/pod-product-compliance
Lightning Source LLC
Chambersburg PA
CBHW031558210526
45464CB00003B/1330